Praise for Amy Laessle-Morgan's *Live Wire*

"To be numb is to feel everything in this slice of jaded Americana which starts in the nineties where 'the shadows had already learned to cling' to the quiet, knowing acknowledgement of current bitter times, 'they voted yes on poison and called it progress'. Visceral; alive with impact and history on the human soul, Laessle-Morgan paints faded flamingos and winter light which never really arrives in a flicker of matches both above ground and under water. Sounds alight on the reader; imagery is curious, gorgeous, rooted in the body and popular culture. Words collide forming mellifluous compounds both whole and incomplete. Meanings are arrived at sitting across the table from grief weighed down by indifferent loves. This collection holds your hand whilst flicking your wrist to release it. The afterglow of its impact is felt long after. Assured, burned, incendiary, a rare talent."

—Emma Conally-Barklem, author

"These poems trace the muscle memory of longing and loss, the intimate ruin of adolescent desire and haunted landscapes of a city's collapse and the body forced to remember it. The applause may fade in time but some dust never truly settles."

—Scott Laudati, author of *Camp Winapooka*
(Bone Machine, Inc.)

"Amy Laessle-Morgan proves with *Live Wire* not only to be a prolific poet, but also the caretaker of forgotten things. Whether it's picking up shavings of nostalgia from a neglected song, or the rotted yet still beating heart of a condemned building, Amy delivers strong impactful imagery while leaving a place at the table for the enigma

—Guy Cramer, writer

"From 'Conduction' to 'Resistance,' 'Current' to 'Ground,' the 'Surge' of gut-punching emotions in *Live Wire* takes the reader on a personal journey of love, loss, memories, and grief. Amy Laessle-Morgan has created another beautifully relatable poetry collection. Her use of imagery and sensory detail bring her writings to life. 'The Yellow Outside,' one of my favorites, tore at my heart and forced me to face my own unresolved grief. And when she wrote, 'I'll write one last poem on a crumpled-up receipt and swear–I didn't write it for you,' I wanted to scream, 'Yes, you did!'"

Terry Hojnacki, Founder & Editor-in-Chief,
Sterling Script: A Local Author Collection

LIVE WIRE

AMY LAESSLE-MORGAN

LIVE WIRE

ISBN: 979-8-218-89854-0

Library of Congress Control Number: 2025927841

Presented by:
Neon Sparrow Press ©
Royal Oak, MI
FIRST EDITION

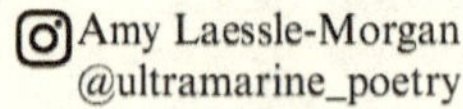

@ultramarine_poetry

PREFACE

"I would like, if I may, to take you on a strange journey."
-*The Rocky Horror Picture Show*

I've carried that opening line around for years like a good luck charm. It always makes me smile to myself when I think, how did I get here and while writing this collection it seemed to be the perfect opening line for this book of poetry you're about to embark on. You see, the Rocky Horror Picture Show wasn't just a movie to me—it was a ritual, a dare, a little permission slip to be weird, loud, desirous, alive. I love the camp, the glamour, Tim Curry's dangerous elegance, the whole glorious thing.

When grief arrived, I found myself returning to that idea of it being such a strange journey—you don't get to choose the door you're pushed through; you only choose whether you keep walking through it. It is these memories that I thought about while writing this. Not only about the shape of grief but the older parts of what shaped me.

Live Wire comes from what followed: survival not as recovery, but continuity. The years after the condolence calls stop. The era when grief is no longer an emergency but more ambient. These poems were written farther out and from much deeper down.

If I've learned one thing, it's that reshaping is not the same as healing. The work has been less "closure" than repair: soldering, steady hands, flux and fire, the willingness to breathe through the faint metallic sweetness of what's burning off. The poems in this book live at the workbench of that process. They test connections and blow fuses. They draw new lines when the old ones won't carry the load. They don't attempt to sanctify pain or prettify it. They try to wire it honestly into the house I still live in.

This is not a book about closure but instead a record of what keeps pulsing, what flickers back on and what refuses to go dark. Wherever these poems find you, thank you for being here—for following the lines, for holding a little of this current with me.

And one last nod to *RHPS*, I don't think I'd be a writer if I didn't at least subconsciously hold onto "*Don't dream it, be it.*"

"And thus by degrees was lit, halfway down the spine, which is the seat of the soul, not that hard little electric light which we call brilliance, as it pops in and out upon our lips, but the more profound, subtle and subterranean glow."

—Virgina Woolf, *A Room of One's Own*

THE CONTENT

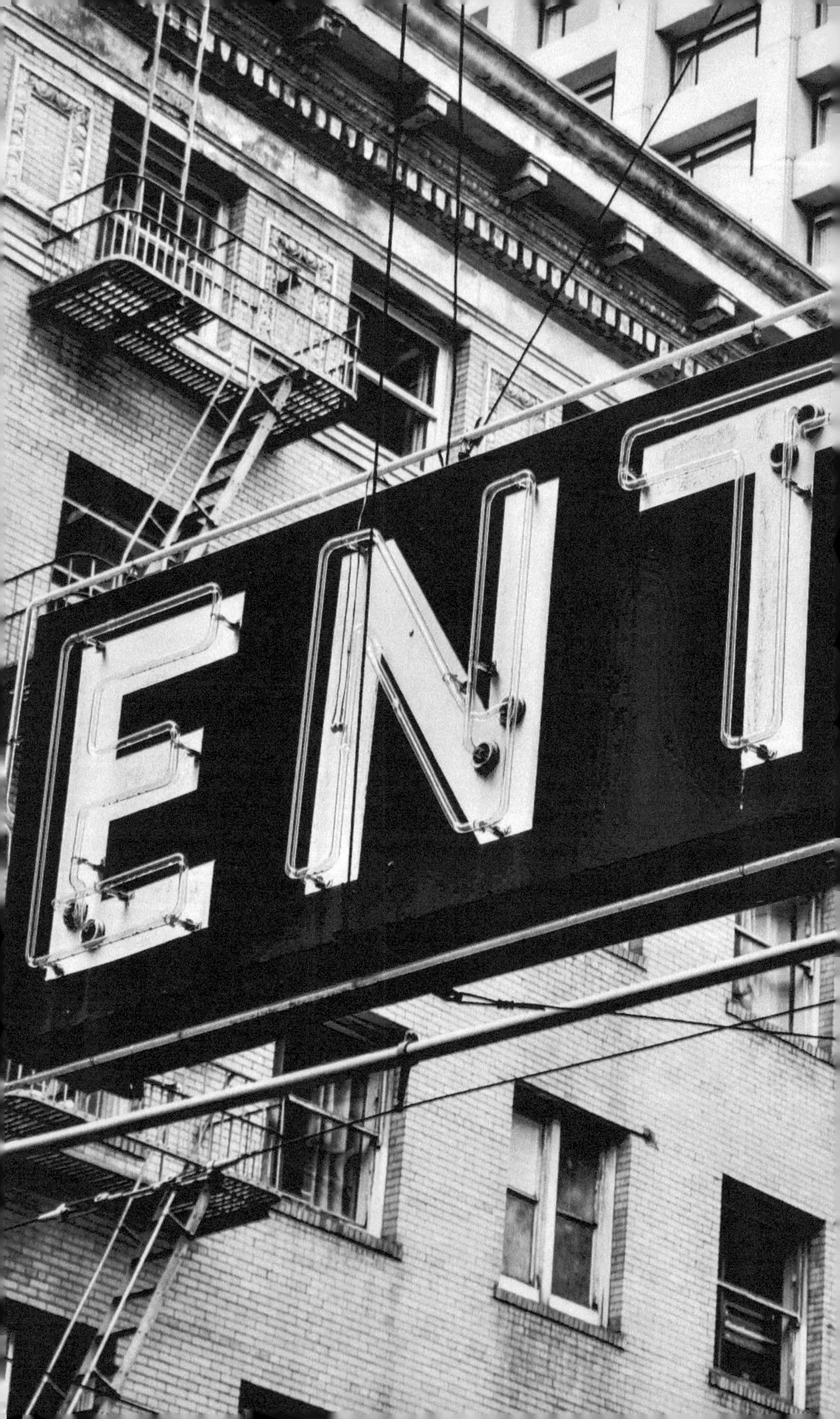
ENT

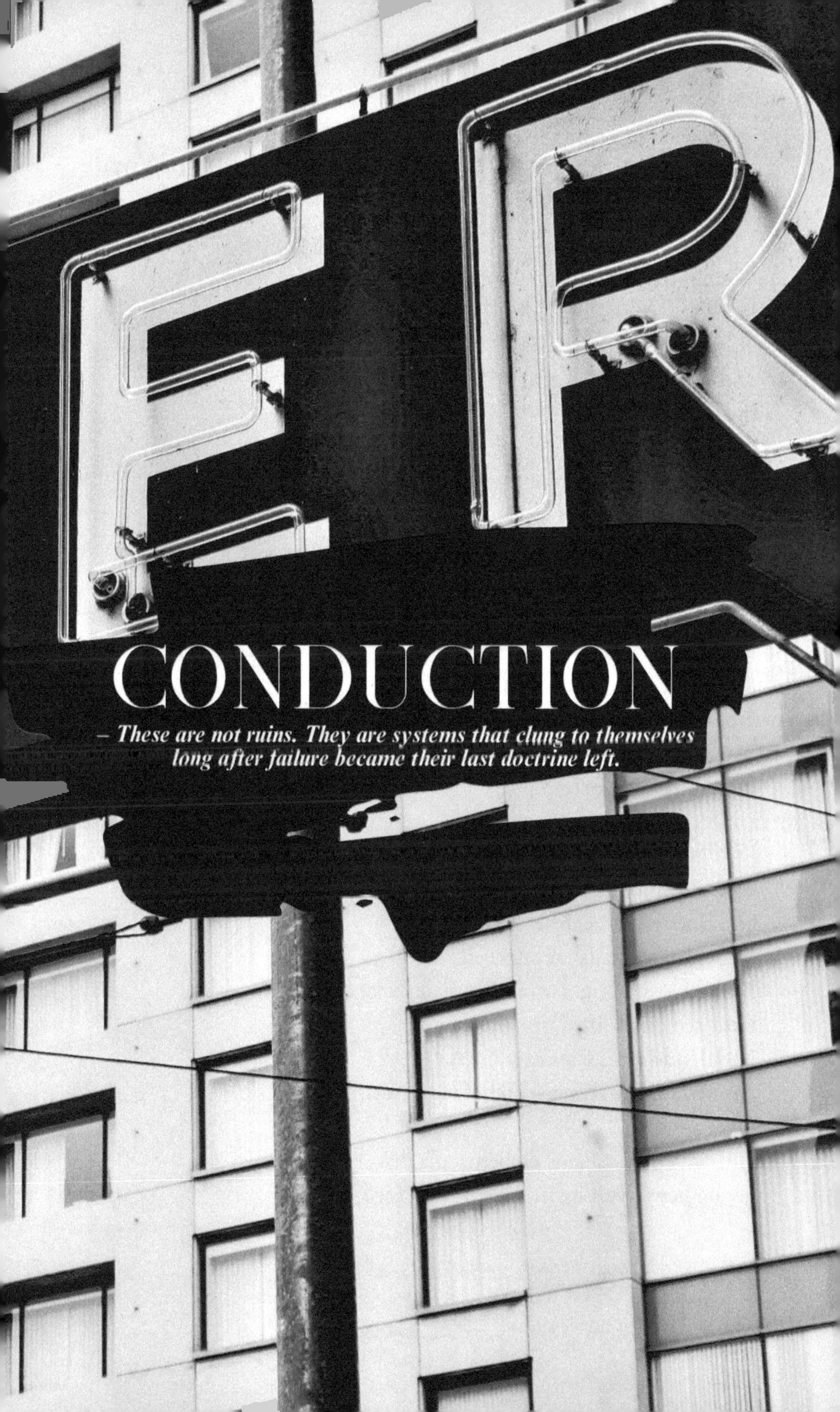

CONDUCTION

– These are not ruins. They are systems that clung to themselves long after failure became their last doctrine left.

This Is an Ekphrastic Poem, but I Don't Want You to Know

Certain truths resist the mouth
like thresholds or endings.
To name them is trespass
and yet, each time I enter the room
the dam breaks
and I weep
not performatively, not even privately
but in the way old buildings collapse
incrementally
then all at once.

My face
tear-slick, varnish-closeup.
Not delicate, but industrial.
The pipes bursting behind the walls
gutters vomiting rivers.

Saltwater blurs the coordinates
where memory ends
and floodplain begins.
Knuckles white as architecture.
Frank Lloyd Wright would've hated me.
I am not clean-lined or cantilevered.
I am load-bearing sorrow
painted in the wrong shade of restraint.

Girl with bad dreams & better playlists
giving new meaning to *A Season in Hell.*

dropout philosopher—
bedroom borrower—

The room: Apollonian in stillness
but what breaks loose inside me: Dionysian.
A tongue fluent in the grammar of exit wounds
making pain look like art.

A frequency just south of memory
brushed into air
like lacquer.
You could call it music, sure
but only because you've bled from experience.
It's more like resonance-induced rupture—
sympathetic collapse.

It's transference, yes
it's also sacred geometry
and naming doesn't stop skin
from leaning towards
frequencies of longing
low, relentless
breaking open.

Again.
Again.

Not for rescue
but witness.
An architect
who can stomach
the collapse.

Cherry Vinyl Motown

I. Side A

A tongue
stained Michigan cherry
from a roadside stand off M-53.
Summer's first sweat
all lemonade-pulped air
syruped with June and lawnmower exhaust
when the lake is still too cold
but everyone jumps in anyway
and cicadas rattle at dusk like loose pearls in a pillbox.

"Tracks of My Tears" threads through me
like needlepoint grief.
Its backbeat finds me between sprinkler arcs
between my shoulder blades
in hips that remember Motown
it spills
pours through the mesh screen door
drips into my ear.

There is something about lyrics
that have slept in your chest since girlhood
like strawberries softening on the counter
till they surrender into jam
till sweetness ferments
till juice stains the wooden cutting board.

I was raised on four-part harmonies.
Smokey's falsetto was the only kind of religion I understood
a psalm I could sway to.

This is where the ache was conceived
in gauzy kitchen light slanting across linoleum
my mother swaying in her slippers
worn thin at the heel.
I watched her move alone
held by melodies no one else could see.

And I want to be held.
And I want someone to hold onto.

II. Side B

My fingers pine to curl around his shoulder
and play the B-sides of unfinished questions.
I sense the tremor
not in his spine
but in the misstep
he doesn't know I felt.
The music enters
like a slow inheritance
inside the deep hum of a bassline
that parts the sternum.

This is how we pass grief
you and I, back and forth—
hand to shoulder
cheek to jaw
palm to pulse

like a glass filled with heartbreak too warm to drink
my mouth on the rim, then yours, then mine again
never asking whose sorrow it is
only knowing it tastes familiar.

You say nothing
and that feels right.
I close my eyes because it's easier to pretend we're not inside
a pain that's hereditary
slow and half-fermented.

There's a kind of steady mercy in 4/4 time.
His hand at my back
not guiding, more like tethering
as if afraid I might slip into the music
and never find my way out.

I notice myself wondering
if he knows
what he's touching.

I press my cheek to his shoulder
not because I trust him, but because the song understands a truth
I've spent years trying to unlearn.

Sometimes
grief needs to be danced with
until it stops leading.

His thumb brushes my back.
I think of cold linoleum floors and press in—closer than I should
because the song is ending, and I've never been good
at letting things go quietly.

Jefferson Ave.

The chorus blurs / to steel-wool snowfall.
I hover my thumb above the dial / searching for a voice
that can survive the distance between towers.
Jefferson unspools beside Lake St. Clair
a sheet of pewter breathing under mansion-dented wind.
I drove babies here when they rattled with colic
engine thrumming lullabies around their cries.
And later, when the house filled with daylight-shaped worry,
I came here alone.
On the far shore someone hangs light-boxes in the reeds
an installation that resembles a delicate veil
lenses blooming with picture-show flicker of things too small to pity:
thread-thin rotifers braiding a future out of dead algae
bacteria sipping rust from drowned anchor chain.
Whole republics eating, dividing, remaking the dark
while we measure survival by headlights and hailstorms.
I park where the asphalt gives itself to sand
through the heft of every body I have ferried
across these night miles.
Wind climbs the antenna, whispering its seabed algorithms.
Somewhere the—no longer babies—
dream of walk-up apartments and faraway riots of full-moon dalliances.
I close my eyes and feel whole cities of plankton
flaring beneath icy edges
patient, innumerable, faithful decay and return.
If there is such a thing as gentleness, it is microbial:
an endless undoing that keeps letting us begin again.
I sit until Jefferson's traffic thins to tailpipe-wind
until the water folds its metal wings into itself
and I drive home through the veil—invisible
that holds even broken music together.

Caller No. 3

He assures me you won't read this
but encourages me to write
because silence, like rot
is not passive.
It proliferates.

To me you were all summer skin and borrowed names.
I was the one who stayed
both louder and longer.
Foolishly. Faithfully. Fact.

I nod when he mentions *the shadow*
like I haven't been living in it for years.

He says *archetype*
I hear *altar.*
He says *anima*
and I forget how to sit still
his eyes are
blue
like lake water when no one's swimming in October
clean, yet deep.
I wonder what's drowned there
and whether it ever tried to rise.

Sometimes I cross my legs, then uncross them
then regret the choreography of my body entirely.

He says *integration* and I think of hands

the quiet grammar inside of wrists.
He always waits.
He's incredibly good at waiting.
I wonder if he's good at it with everyone
or just with me
and then hate myself for wondering.
I pretend I don't care
but I do.
I care in a way that makes my mouth taste like metal.

He calls it *unconscious defense.*
I say *I guess so.*
I don't say: *you look so calm when you're listening.*

I tell myself I'm over it.
I say it like a prayer.
I say it like a dare.
I taste dust
every time he says *go on.*

I am Caller Number 3
but this time I say nothing.
Let the line go dead
let them wonder where I went.

He wants to go back
(but I never left)
to the beginning
or some cracked part of it.
He doesn't use the word dig
but I still feel
the shovel rupture soil
under each of his careful questions.

He thinks he's gentle.
Maybe he is.
I nod.
I'm good at nodding.
It looks like agreement but mostly means
please don't look too hard at me.

I don't know how to walk backward in a straight line.
My history is a hallway with bad lighting.

He talks about dreams.
I lie.
Say I don't remember them.
(I do, every one)
Last night I walked barefoot through a field of withered camellias
and every bloom had a mouth
and every mouth was trying to tell me something
I already knew.

He asks me what I need
as if I have the map.
As if I haven't been
digging through unmarked graves
with my bare hands.

I need what I never learned to ask for.
I need not to be asked.
I need the silence to know me.

1
ABC 2
DEF 3
GHI 4
JKL 5
6
PRS 7
8 TUV
9 WXY
0 OPERATOR
AREA CODE 313

Love Me Two Times (Driving East)

I drove through New England like it still held answers
returning to the first tender suture of coastline
with hopes it might remember my name.

A pale-yellow sun punctuated Route 2 as
scrub oaks twisted skyward.
Brambles and bayberry crowded the edge of the road.
Cedar and salt grass tangled in the wind.

Every which way I looked
spirits clung
to stone walls
to clapboard houses
to hollowed-out wounds of a splintered heart.

The Doors' "Love Me Two Times"
rattled the windshield
dragging me back to sixteen again
knees pulled to my chest on a well-loved thrift store couch and
my friend's older brother, alive, in a basement
backlit by Christmas lights
talking about Baudelaire
while leaning against their dented washer.
He didn't see me studying his
cigarette embering slow between his fingers.

There's something slightly volatile
housed in his careless posture
and I realize I'm the one moving closer.
His blond hair
falls wild around his face
and it is beautiful.

Leather jacket in summer
the closest incarnation
of Jim Morrison in the flesh—
not in looks but the way
you felt like you were one word
from being incinerated or saved.
Pothos before I knew what to do with it.

I watch him
like a movie I'm not allowed to see.
He really didn't care for me
and I can't say that I blame him.
But I still search
for outlines shaped like him
in men who speak in half-lost verses
who wear the end of the world
written across a T-shirt.

Miles flickered past.
A vigil of headlamps swept the dark
offering up small, recurring memories
until I circled back
past churches older than the Constitution
through towns that sound like
old ferry schedules and closed doors:
Chilmark
Swansea
Orleans

Melancholia is a muscle and
I've built mine on repetition.
It feels almost holy now.
Like loyalty to pain
because it's the only thing that never walks out.

"Love me two times"
because the first was rehearsal.
Because the second still won't be enough.
Because severence is a salt lick
and my tongue is worn raw
from trying to name it
softer.

Detroit, October 24, 1996 — Fall of the Hudson Building

They said it would be clean
5:47 p.m.— *to minimize shadows*
as if the dark was the problem.

Hudson's was already dead.
Nineteen stories of
boarded-up-red-brick-ghost-breathed-mold
a mausoleum for everything we were told to want.

When the charges fired
I watched each floor implode vertebra by vertebra.

I watched it fall.
I watched it fall.
I watched it fall
and I learned what endings sound like:

seismic.

Choreographed obliteration.
Revitalization as desecration.

The only thing I'd seen fall harder than that store
was my grandfather two years prior.
He crumpled slow, like a church steeple
surrendering from the inside out.
Hudson's was swift
but the sound was the same.

Windows shattered six blocks away.
Dust spilled like afterbirth across streets
slow, pale particulate tidal waves haloed the skyline
rolled past Campus Martius
and curled over I-375.
The new Ash Wednesday for non-believers.

We watched it come.
We didn't run
and still
it sought us.
It took less than thirty seconds to erase a century.

There we stood on Woodward Avenue
nineteen, twenty, twenty-five, flannel shirts, no coats
choosing October's firelight more than fearing its burn
lungs prepared to archive
whatever came next.
My boyfriend said
"This is history."
I paused Portishead playing in my discman and said
"Have we learned nothing from Rome?"

The people cheered.
Cheered like ruin was a parade.
Cheered like absence was finally affordable.
Cheered like their grandmother hadn't
bought a bra on the sixth floor in 1952.

But I didn't cheer.
I held my shirt over my face, tasting copper and chalk
asbestos and apparitions wondering what the debris would do to us—
I still wonder that now.

"It's harmless"
they said
but I still cough randomly on late November evenings.
Some days
I still taste the mortar.
Some days
I still feel the wreckage in my chest.
Body as witness to the
somaesthetic ache that lives under skin
and inside my bloodstream.

They gave us the implosion
but not the cleanup crew.
They handed us rubble
and expected applause
and they got it.

The people clapped.
The people clapped.
The people clapped
when the charges detonated
and learned what endings really sound like.

You can't sweep away that kind of dust.

Swing 199X

It began with a sound.
The slow cry of a chain
half-bird, half-gate
like violins in a French film
under a rust-crossed yoke of skybars.

I remember well
the scorched-rubber curve of the swing seat
mid-July
summer of 199X
sweat-welded to the backs of my thighs
skin peeled like a lunchbox orange
hot but not unpleasant
like I was meant to endure it.

My knees skinned
throned in orbit.
A sticky pack of cherry-cola Now and Laters
glued to the cotton lining of my pocket
artificial sweetness and Yellow No. 5 dissolved
into something I couldn't name.

I thought
if I kicked hard enough
the sky might part
like velvet stage curtains
and I could disappear
stage-left
into someone less anxious.

My heart dropped
to the bottoms of my feet
and I liked it
feared it
felt it anyway.

Believed I could outrun
the shadows that had already learned
to cling by age eleven.

I kicked
harder, like my life depended on it.
And I rose
tore through the sky
like it might forgive me
this blur of girl-gravity-sugar.
Up there
I wasn't afraid
of falling.
I welcomed it.
I let go
flew, flailed
a blur of limbs
my body a bright mistake
hurling back to earth.

The landing was not clean.
The mulch split at the impact
my palms bit gravel
dirt flooded my mouth
the sting immediate
hot and sharp.

Pain rushed in
full-bodied
and I tasted every small wound that had made me.

They gave me panic
but this—
this I gave myself.

And it sang.

And it was mine.

And it was honest.

Postcards from Nowhere

There are towns whose buildings understand entropy better
than we ever learned.
Structures engineered not to endure
but to gesture, to promise
to shine a brief flare off windows
against the unseen.

You feel it in the forged steel
that forgets its own vocation
and joists that sigh like old men
losing familiar names.

Architecture—at its root—was never merely shelter;
it was assertion
an arrogance of angles against the elements.
The Archē, the beginning, origin, first principles.

We raised monoliths to beckon the divine downward and
factories to kneel before the great humming god of capitalism.
Now both subside with the same silent erasure.

In these towns the profitable
have long since departed
the way of sandhill cranes
to more lucrative climates.

I walk these streets to trace cracks of building plaster—
fault lines on a body trying (and failing)
to forget its trauma.

These are not ruins.
They are systems that clung to themselves
long after failure became their last doctrine left.
No one razes them; no one remembers how to let go
of what once felt inevitable as breath.

I'm in love with architecture because
it is the purest form of truth.
It holds absence with unsettling honesty.

People stay because structure—
though fractured, sagging, almost ashamed
is familiar.

I know how familiarity
becomes gospel
habit, existence.

These are not ghost towns
but I move through them ghost-like—
a haunted blueprint still lived in
insisting on a half-lit relevance.

And still I write postcards from nowhere
and sign my name
because nowhere still lives inside me.

The Garden Sessions

(i. opening notes)

In the delicate hum of not-quite-June
we sat on the back patio
between red and white quince
and the sigh of blue-leaning hyacinth
fluttering in the breeze
like they'd once been kissed
and never fully recovered.

Christine felt like a sanctuary in muslin.
I watched her cat thread through the lilies
tail flicking like an exclamation point.
I wasn't quite ready to speak.

The roses sagged in that romantic way
like mourning you hide internally but
looks beautiful when someone else finally sees it.

She spoke in the muted click of cat claws on porchwood
and poured the tea into a chipped cup—
the one with the pale green rim
and hairline crack across the base.
Her hands were always so still
rested on the saucer as if they were thinking.

I traced the veins of an English daisy
while she whispered something about time
how healing erupts within petals
or pink noise just before a sentence breaks.

She called grief “a feral thing
that sleeps in your hair
and wakes up when the wind changes.”
How love doesn’t vanish
just reshapes
into the soft refusal
to stop checking the door.

She talked about how “there are people who live inside us
like fishhooks—
barbed, beautiful, difficult to remove
without tearing something essential.”
The garden bloomed around our pauses and
I found myself conjuring your name
without saying it.

(ii. the earth remembers)

She told me once—not as flattery—
that I had a way of drawing things in.
Not quite myth—more like earth-mother
nurturing, with soil on her hands
and that’s why they came—
the ones with broken compasses
and bright faces
always hungry
never ready
arriving like birds in the wrong season, confused by the warmth.
“You’re like the soil—you’ll hold anything if it presses hard enough.”
And I laughed, I think
or the cat did or the wind brushed the porch
like a memory I mistook for joy.

Sometimes I feel made of rainwater, moss
and the sting behind it—not gentle, not powerful, just old.
Old in a way that scares people because it makes them feel young again
and no one wants to be young unless someone is there to hold it.

(iii. the last of the light)

October leaves were letting go, their fall a rust-colored ballet of loss.
Only the marigolds still burned in the corners—
fists of orange defiance clinging to what had once been lush.

The tea was darker now, spiced.
Christine wore a wool shawl the color of woodsmoke
and the cats stayed curled instead of pacing.
I didn't say much—there wasn't much to say.
We'd named the ache so many times it had grown tired of being called.

I asked her if healing meant forgetting.
She gazed at the garden then at me and said
"No, it means letting memory be a place you walk through
without the fear of being devoured."

Somewhere under all that green and gold and gone
I felt the smallest part of me untangle.
She had always made room for what was wild—poured the tea
left the gate unlatched and I came back again and again
thinking she was the garden's keeper.

But I see it now.
She was tending me
and I
I was the thing
blossoming.

Midwest Prophecy

The Indiana sky held its breath that summer.
Fairmount was 97° and counting.
Everything sweating
the windows, the road, the inside of my thighs.

We were sun-sick and newlywed
driving on fumes and vending machine sugar
because James Dean once lived somewhere near corn.

A pilgrimage
to a red-brick town
where the post office remained proud of its hours and
sidewalks remembered the shape of Memorial Day parades.

We stopped at Casey's for red carnations
for Jimmy.
Everyone here still calls him Jimmy
that makes him theirs.
I wore a pale blue dress
with the straps that kept slipping from
gravity or omen, I can't be sure
and you took my picture
with that click-wind plastic camera
cheap lens, soft light.
Click. Wind. Click.

He's beloved there.
You feel it in the careful trim of cemetery grass
and the eyes of the cashier who wrapped our carnations.

They speak of the way he smiled in the cafeteria line
and once skipped gym.
Like he's still walking somewhere down Main
and not at the top of the hill
his name clean and shiny from years
of worship and residue:
hands and Marlboros and dimes and
the smear of red lipstick drying in the sun.

I knelt on a baptism of heat-struck grass
years before I understood the kind of scorch grief leaves
and wrote a confession on the back of our hotel receipt
crimson ink dotting the "i" with a heart I wasn't embarrassed by yet.
Folded the paper into something small enough to hide
and slipped it into the soil beside his name
a seed I pretended could take root.
As if the ground keeps secrets.
As if boy saints bothered to read cursive.

We were happy then
or something dressed like it.
Death still felt romantic
like something we could borrow and give back.

How cleanly cruel the first thing to fade
was what we thought would last.
There was nothing sacred in that Indiana soil of red-bricked devotions
where we knelt like believers
until we were shown a prophetic truth
when the flowers wilted and the photos never developed
that *"nothing gold can stay."*

200
V

CURRENT

—There was always something burning—toast, bridges, the last good version of me I kept resuscitating with mouth-to-mouth-watering memory.

Butterscotch

Somewhere between the amberblush streetlight of Division
and the butterscotch stain on the back of my throat
there was a glasslike moment
nearbent
but not yet breaking.

Half-formed, honeydrunk on the hour
slipping past the soft machinery of becoming
unbecoming
rewinding
rethreading.

Warm, butterfat air washing in subtle
breathing through the cracked window taxicab
teacuplight broken open on my cheek
murmuring *nothing is permanent*
except the way we almost changed.

There was always something burning—
toast
bridges
the last good version of me I kept resuscitating
with mouth-to-mouth-watering memory.

Tonight, I'll wear that dress you loved
in the color of skinbrushed apologies
while the past rides shotgunsilent
adjusting the mirror like it still matters how I see myself

because when mirrors grow honest
the corridors echo less
as everyone pours out.

Let us go then
through goldblood hours
where no one teaches you how to bleed pretty
not in the swanpale wrist pressed
to cold porcelain tile way
half-lit in someone else's forgetting.

You learn it knees to marble
cheek to linoleum
in radio silence buzzing through your teeth
playing love songs that didn't learn the language.

He liked it leaning in disrepair
so I sucked the ghostsweet butterscotch slow.
I let it split goldenglass hard and sharp
the bloom red blooming
behind teeth
a salty flood.
It cut me
but I didn't spit it out.

I kept it—
I kept it all.

Wellfleet, 24 Frames Per Second

The screen at the Wellfleet Drive-In
has seen more endings than most lives
spilling silver flicker onto windshields
since the summer of '57.
Tonight, the heat lightning dots out Morse code
unzipping the sky.

A childhood reflex counted the seconds between thunder
before I understood distance doesn't dilute pain—
it only names how long it takes to arrive.
Now it glows at the margins of the screen in a kind of perseverance
light, of course, cannot keep.

A violet aperture
slices June's humid fabric into long, cinematic ribbons.
I think it's almost beautiful.
You'd say, "it's just the humidity" and I smile
when I think how we both love the color purple
as though color alone was the only thing holding the plot together.

(The rest has been trimmed and spliced
for continuity)

I can feel the phantom-heat of your knee by the gearshift.
Color ascending my skin like Rosa rugosa climbing the dunes
an unruly magenta that sweetens the air
even as it devours the shoreline.
The locals will warn you it leaves a mark
on anything careless enough to brush against it.

An Anderson film, because it always is
running on loop in powdered pastels.
Candy-colored anguish trimmed intricately fits the frame
the way whimsy dresses wounds in the colors of love
that particular lavender
that marine green.
Every choice deliberate.
Each frame immaculate
as the opening credits keyed to bathroom tiles.
The whole thing symmetrical, tragic, held in
which is precisely what makes it
so strangely palatable.

Michael Cera is kindness in khakis
cradling a borrowed Norwegian accent
with the rehearsed sincerity of a Provincetown busker.

I lift my arm through the projector beam
folding it into a map of the Cape.
Wellfleet is the tender forearm
easy to cut, slow to heal
where young men once drafted poems
and vanished
into silence
or fire
or Manhattan.

It's well past midnight as
end credits roll up and evaporate into nothing.
The sky re-fastens its buttonstars elegantly
as if nothing had ever
come undone.

December 2nd

Dear X,

Grief kept peering over my shoulder tonight
telling me to make this about *her*.
Write me down, she said
spell out every inch you lost.
But I refused her.

Instead, I wrote about the high school crush I had in homeroom
in all caps, black pen digging into the page
hands shaking
but the line stayed.

It felt like a tiny riot
on cheap paper
one word standing up
against the whole weight of what's gone.

I wouldn't sign my name under it
wouldn't let anyone say
I belonged to them.

Why should the dark get the credit
for what keeps refusing to die?

Opaline

My heart
has become a small outlaw of an organ
savors every recklessness
like black sequins drifting across bathwater
gone gray and circling the drain.

How I long to be more opaline—
to refract, not reflect.
To become the thing light has to work its way through
slant and split around.

I'm always telling some stranger or ceiling or notebook
that if I could just tilt the glass right
they would finally see what I really am.

Not transparent,
not brick-solid either
but that milky in-between
that refuses to give up
the whole story all at once.

I am not here to be read clean.
I am here to be held up
opal-troved
just water, silica and voids
throwing off color
as if seeing were believing.

The Yellow Outside

April waltzed in like a well-intended letter
hips swaying and full of herself
like the frostbite didn't require amputating vital parts.

Still, the robins have returned with downy chests
to rebuild everything winter has gutted
something small and certain in the bend of the eaves.

The buttercups
burst with audacity
pressing color against glass
like they were trying to get inside
unaware the air still bites
at anything trying to open.
They don't seem to care
I'm not ready for beautiful beginnings right now.

In the rustle of first-born leaves
I glimpse the quiet nod of someone
who knows why I stare at the sky too long and hesitate at doorways
the way I swallow panic like supper
and call it ceasefire.

These tragedy-braced hands
live with me now in gestures
the way I fix my collar
the way I press pause right before the part
that always wrecks me.

I didn't flinch
when the buttercups came
no one thinks twice about their bright little toxins.

I cracked the window to let them see me and said
If I ever open, it'll be scar tissue drinking in the sun
and if I never do
at least I withstood
what arrived to unmake me.

To Split the Sky

I took a drive this morning down that same busted vein of road
split-lipped asphalt cutting through
the heart of mundane suburbs—past tired homes
and rusting mailboxes.

It felt different this time.
You always seem like the horizon
burning bright—almost otherworldly.
The sky opened
tinted in shades of rose and ember
like Turner once painted.

I chased the burn of sunrise
its fire licked the edges of earth
reminding me
how I used to ignite when you said my name.

My tires thrummed against
lane lines ticking past
as the world blinked itself awake.

The road blurred and
I wanted that hit again
the way your kiss
sank into sun-starved skin
like mercy.
Like menace.
Like the kind of danger
you never survive
but still beg for
with both hands open.

Isn't it enough to be
the horizon—to be the brink
of space drawn taut between yes and yet?

What a quiet disaster, this not-knowing
as you move through the day untouched
while strangers reset their whole lives
by the glow that trails behind you.

Palimpsest

My darling ache-machine
the record-player skips
in that loop-looped little chime of not-quite-love
or not-quite-over
like it knew me in more presentable skin
and sodium vapor air
lyrics that mock the shape of missing
the way the body swallows back a name it used to borrow

On the sill
bonebutton (cracked)
grapes of glass (4)
& the sun like citrus pulp lemonlight
bleeding through sheer-washed curtains
the thinnest drapery known to womanhood

My etymon is full
of aftertaste
and
needlethread lulls
a confusion that alphabetizes itself
in hash-marks
some call it bad timing
I call it déjà vu with bruises
I am palimpsest
overwritten
me
on me
on me

Pierce Stocking Drive

I drove to the top of the world
or what passed for it at the top-of-the-mitten.
I can't seem to escape sorrow fossilized into myth.
The legend of a mother bear
turned powdered-quartz mountain of mourning calcifies the dunes.
The lake swallows her lineage like it swallows years.
It seems even God at times forgets
to unmake what bereavement built
and we—sentimentalists in linen and sunglasses
call it a view.

The lake looked tropical
the color of dream-lagoon postcards
but it was never meant to.
The quagga mussel
latched onto ships from the Black Sea
and filtered out truth
leaving water but stealing marrow
from Lake Michigan's food chain.

We called it beautiful
because the lie was photogenic
which felt poetic, if not quite fair.

I watched children cannonball into the parasitic aftermath
and thought it funny no one bothered to ask what it used to look like.

I'm no stranger to insides turning tropic.
Look how well I filter.
You could drink my stories and never choke
but there's always a price paid
for clean water.

You'd think the Midwest couldn't seduce you
but it does.
The ghost of manifest destiny sweats through its skin.
Grain elevators leer like monuments
to some forgotten eroticism of labor.

Maybe Socrates would appreciate the irony
of dense forests flanked with maple and hemlock.
After all, clarity never came without a little poison.

I sat there on the beach near Pierce Stocking Drive
watching water pretend to be the Caribbean.
Just another invasive soft-bodied thing
pretending I belong here.

And what a thing it is
to be both
the parasite
and
the view.

The Lights Are Still On

I didn't mean to fall asleep with the lamp on overhead
unflattering
catching every rogue crease in the sheets
and every tiny failure of skin.

There is nothing to be solved.
No verdicts.
No plans for tomorrow.
Just this mattress hugging our curves.
Two tired people
lying parallel.
And somehow it feels extravagant to be this unguarded
eyes half-closed
face bare
stomach soft
my knee finding the warmth of your calf without asking permission
every flaw on display.

I could reach up
flick the switch
make us prettier in the dark
but that would cheapen it.

This is the luxury—
to be bodies bathed in light
everything seen, surrendering so easily
that even small things
like turning lights off
feel too far away to matter.

VECH
RICU
VICU
VAGI
TRC 2
TRC 3
TRCS
TRCR
AUTO MANU
REARM
APPEL PREP.
PC1

VATR
PORE POTR
VAEV
RIN 1
SURGE
VPBA
—Craving ignition is chemical.
It's not romance. It's thermodynamics.
PC2
REPO

Ruin Me Buddy Holly

I have a type.
Apparently, it's men with horn-rimmed glasses.
1950s, thick-framed, Buddy Holly–adjacent.
Less fashion, more necessity
soft blinks, harder truths
"these help me see" kind.
The cost of clearness paid in syntax bent like the will of a saint.

There's something about a man who frames his vision through lenses
and a lifetime of hesitation.
Esquivel, James Dean, Rivers Cuomo
Joaquin Phoenix—
all frames and too lovely.

I like to watch him remove them in the evening
how he folds the temples carefully
and sets them on the nightstand
only to rub
the bridge of his nose.
He cleans the lenses like lab work.
Prescribed restraint.
Optometry of intimacy.
Interpreting the world in millimeters
through curved glass and conditional trust.

Measure me in diopters.
Evaluate for curvature.
Declare me nonstandard.
Circle aberrations in red pen.

Let him write: +1.75 emotionally uncorrected
and try to fix the way I scatter light
like I am dangerous in high definition.

I'm not saying horn-rimmed men are better.
I'm just saying
when they take off their glasses
slowly, carefully
like disarming a bomb
it's because they know love is always rigged
but risk the detonation.

And I know it's real because the glass hazes chalk-white
before the apology remembers its consonants
like a getaway car
still purring
lights off
heart revved
stepping towards me
letting the shape of me arrive in him
unedited
full exposure.

Maymelt

maymelt all over the hourglass curve
sunspilt, dripslick
on the nape of a neck
you—blurbrushed
soft-spoken
hands
not touching but
hoverwarmed
pre-kiss
pre-words
pre-anything that ends in faultline tension

lilacspill
down the sides of my seeing
a barecalf rub against the greenbristle
of maybegrass
a thought unwinds the hem
of undressed desire
fingers thread through my hair
reverenceruined
lightdripped
your eyes a hush I seek
to sleep inside

shadowdance
flickerframe slow, then fast
a hush hum
until it lands
sinkdeep

your voice—velvetcracked
murmurmilk
swung into the small of my back

we are all lips
and sidelong hunger
a sidewaysness
of petalpulse
a slipping inside

hushhalved
coldpressed between thighskin

then tongueheat
slow, certain
maymelt moves upward
spine-strung
wet with wanting
all around us
the lilacs spilling themselves
without apology

I cling to your shoulder
like it's the last
true surface on earth
you relichold mine
like it's the first

yes
yes
yes

more

Live Wire

Craving ignition is chemical.
It's not romance. It's thermodynamics.
A red phosphorus, powdered glass, sweet-panic hiss
about to become flame.

I want that heat but distrust warmth.
And if I'm still glowing well, maybe the anesthesia was never complete.
Like electricity outrunning sound
by the time the warnings arrive
the skin's already mid-blister.

Voltage spikes in limbic dark
an amygdala ticking like a Geiger counter
of language too messy to mop up the spill on aisle seven.

Fragmentation without resolution
never disappears—it reroutes
slips underground, too hot to touch
wet-copper ground, mouth-close.
A live wire buzzing
with its dimmer switch stuck in the halfway-down position
waiting for someone with damp fingers thumbing through Ovid
mistaking *Metamorphoses* for empathy.

You want to know...
does it still burn where spark once hit flesh?
Then don't ask.
Place your hand to my scorched flesh
and don't call me sentimental
because you know
I still kept the match.

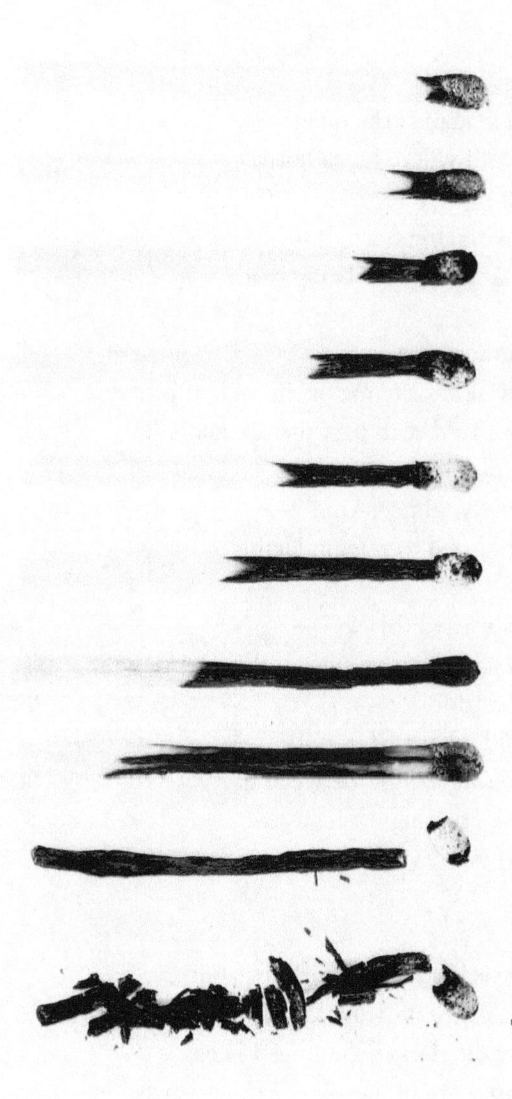

Nameless Grace

In the half-light
I could almost
press my cheek against the quiet.
That held-breath where I was not yet
separate from myself
folded, then worrying open
like a page that knows it's being read.

I was endless there.
Not bound by skin or name or the weight of days.
I kept hoping you'd read past the sentences
past the careful falsities
and dig—politely, almost kindly—
into what I'd buried to remain legible.

I have always waited this way—
inside rooms paneled with unsaid things lining the walls.
If I opened that door
could you hold what rushes out
or would it gather weight between us
swelling into a crossing
neither one of us survives intact?

Even so
I would let myself go down with the ship
for the simple grace of being known
let you follow the darker shadings I keep
feel the full pressure of me—more than words
more than fleeting desire.
But what remains
when both fail?

A soul laid bare
peaceful and full.

I yearn for you to see me as Byron wrote
eloquent beauty
in the silent gasp of evening
when everything glows just enough
to believe it will last forever.

Legend

One unnoticed day
the universe will swallow itself whole
when the last red glow dissolves into sky
and closing moments disband into silence
not even memory will survive the collapse.

And yet, somehow, I know I will still remember
how the world dimmed for a single moment
when I first noticed you across the room
how the nights stretched themselves longer
and I stopped keeping track of time
as if the stars themselves were conspiring to keep me awake
steeped in thoughts of you.

You'd have to unwrite history and change every ending
trace back the ink where my name entered your story
press your mouth to mine
drag the truth from my lips
like an illicit confession
silence the moon and swallow it whole
until its silver searchlight no longer spills through my window.

Even then, I would still whisper your name inside the dark—
still feel it move between one pulse and the next.

Somewhere in another lifetime
I am kissing you at the edge of the universe
as the lights go out one by one,
small bursts of glass and halo
in the loveliest soft-focus dissolve ever filmed.

and for once, we'd exist outside of time.

But here, I live in the aftermath
of what never, almost, nearly was

as if legend could be held—
as if time would allow it.

A Study in Desire

I am breathless, weightless
pressed like an offering against cool iron railing
where night leans too close
hungry for the wreckage
restless as the pulse in my throat.

I like to watch the careful way your eyes trace
the delicate curve of my upper lip where it dips at the center
as if it were at the edge of something forbidden
something meant to be devoured.
We are salt-slick and fever-warm.
I unfasten beneath you
dress slipping like a wayward equinox
legs wrapped tight around your waist
hips meeting hips
spelling want in blunt, urgent flesh-tone syllables
drunk on the hush of a world that does not matter
not here, not now.

Your lips at my throat
I whisper your name like something reverent
like something to kneel before.
Your mouth is warm tangerine
painting murals along my skin
devouring it the way poets devour tragedy
like the bite of nectarine left too long in the sun
dripping down my ribs
pulling me deeper

dragging me under
flesh bursting, amber and glistening.
Sinking within the
vast inescapable sea of you.

A slow, worshiping sway
of orange-blossom-perfumed breeze
exhales into night
sated, yet a little wrecked
knowing it will never taste such honey again.

Selection A11

clickclatter
he knows just how much pressure to give
(a lean and a knowing elbow).
I come loose in that
dropped-from-the-top-shelf kind of way
late-July fluorescent-lit blush
cellophane moan
polyethene breath
refrigerated lust
skinwrap sweating through

rosebite—
the seam of his cheek
remembers the flavor of
coin-slot-sliding offerings

& the incandescence flickers
& the buttons stick
& the tray shudders

candy-shell posed neon inertia
algorithmic, semiotic sheen
unwrapped slow

(red-dye No. 5 melting lacquergloss)

he wants
first bites
ceremony

the sacrament of texture
like etymologies
like sweetness as worship
in the name of
hunger

every time I dissolve
into tongueprint, sugarfilm,
he watches
like it's always the first time
and never enough
breath on glass
slow, hot, fogging the outline of me

I gleam for him
lit mercury
he craves
like he's starving
but insists on silverware
his eyes devour me
before his hands do
two slow blinks
& I melt
like a martyr

clickclatter

selection made

I Said I Had Come for the Apples

I said I had come for the apples
the Ashmead's Kernel, oxidized gold
to feel the weight of them
tight-skinned, Rubenesque, knowledge-wrung
like small truths you name before biting.

The trees were burdened with decadence
limbs bowed in erotic surrender
botany as blasphemy.

Each branch a slow arch
offering primrose-soft-pulp polished to honey
somewhere between thesis
and temptation.

You walked ahead of me
your back framed by late October light
your face refracted shimmers of labradorite in the sun
A blue not of oceans
but of September sapphire
as your cheekbone became iconographic
and your clavicle called for worship.

The rich loam gave slightly beneath my boots
as we stood between mythologies:
the apple as sin
the apple as offering
the apple as pretext
for saying each other's name without consequence.

We spoke in borrowed sentences.
and believed the soul burned green
when aligned with longing.
We were nothing
if not verdant.

I plucked one from the branch
just above your shoulder
but you're the one I want to sink my teeth into.

Apples are all just metaphor
sweet flesh that gives when punctured.
You look toward me all-knowing
like you are the orchard.

After all, desire holds its own dialect.
Tactile.
Paleolithic.
Unpublishable.

The path curved out ahead of us
an autumn road going down
into something we'd name later.
Starlings catalogued the sky
in slow parentheses as
I thought about how Eve wasn't tempted
but curious
and how the brightest hungers
don't starve to stay beautiful
they strive to make surrender
taste like salvation.

I said I had come for apples
but I wanted the wild, overripe orchard
of your body and mind
to understand
what happens
when you swallow fruit
stem
sin
and all.

The Last Renaissance

We have twenty years left
that's what the article said
twenty.
Not a century
not even a gold-belled anniversary.
Twenty summers maybe
or less if the oil sings louder
and oceans rise like women wronged
and every kiss will start to taste like
the brink of extinction.

They gave it a number like it was reasonable.
Twenty more years of museums and mangoes
back-alley bare skin, trembling like final notes
of rooftop rum dripped over moonburnt cheeks
so smooth we won't feel it killing.

We're living inside the fine print until
the sun's just a puddle of birthday candle wax
where I still say please too often
still cross my legs too tight
still wait for permission
still won't make a scene.

Let me go wick-red and wanting
get reckless inside of stairwells
rage against the funeral's procession
etch FOR A GOOD TIME CALL—LIMITED TIME OFFER
inside bathroom stalls.

If this is the last Renaissance
then let me be decadent.
Let me be dangerous.
Let me be mine
in this city haze-tinged pink from the fires of Alberta
with her stockings rolled all the way down—
wildflowers rioting through her concrete seams.

Let us slip into a random Tuesday morning where you smudge
mine in marmalade across my thighs because
even Caravaggio painted in bruises.

We're on a tight schedule—
the stuccoed ceiling is crumbling
shedding pigments of white-gold filigree mirrors.

So let us spill out
like we are the last ruinous things—
like we were always meant to go out
with everything showing.

To Be Known

With the rains came March
not gentle, not penitent
but sharp-limbed and voracious.
A lion with barometric humidity rising in its lungs
rattling the brass fastenings of winter's great coat.

And there I was, laughing upward
hair seized by the storm's quick fingers
tumbling into a passenger seat
with the unruly certainty
of someone who has never belonged
to anything still
and I thought, sharply to myself
Who has ever truly known you
wind-flung, threshold-bold
half-unbuttoned from propriety
bare-shouldered and
translating yourself through five conflicting schools of thought?

Who knows the way your laughter outpaces you
and your eyes flicker like the last streetlight
before dawn, risking exposure?

Who has seen the way your balmy breaths
fog a car window at midnight
parked on asphalt sparkling like Jazz-Age New York
where your guard slipped
and you let someone close enough
unrepentant, unvarnished, unafraid
while you tore your name free like a freshwater-pearl brooch
pin popping white spark pearls ricocheting across the floor mats?

Who truly saw you
not as a silhouette departing
not as an approximation
but as fact
phenomenon
tasting the world without a brake?

Who knows you as you were in that brief, wild hour
when March came in like a lion
and you, astonishingly
did too.

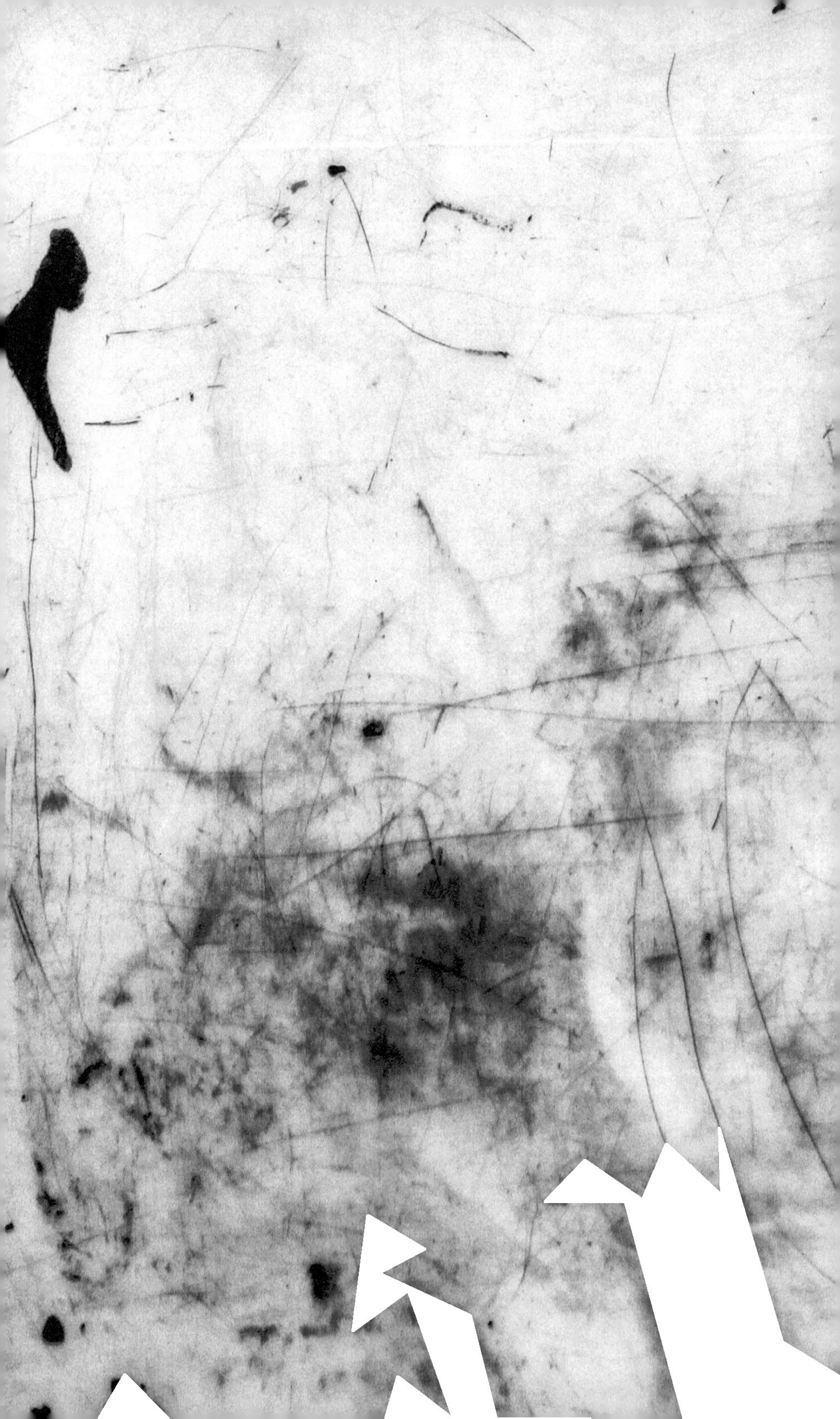

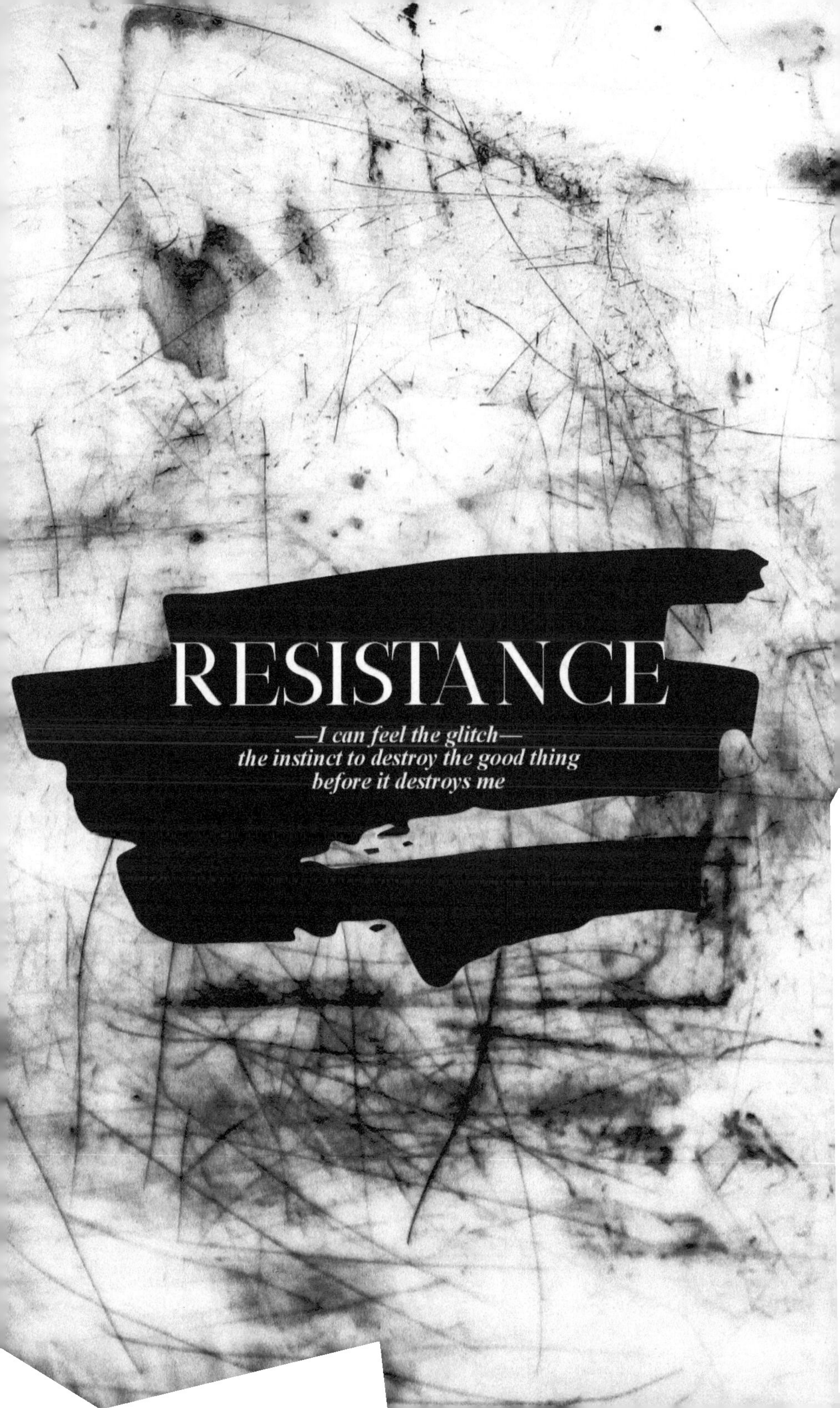
RESISTANCE
—I can feel the glitch—
the instinct to destroy the good thing
before it destroys me

Catch-22

There's no way to win here.
The system is always rigged
a leap of faith outfitted with flimsy parachutes
guaranteed to fail mid-fall.
Hold tighter, it slips faster.
Let go, you plummet.

We carry it like soldiers
marching circles around the past
to a cadence of silent resignation.
A reflection so familiar it burns
because it's mine as much as it's yours.

We are caught in an endless campaign
in a world full of casualties and contradictions.
I know it too well to despise it
and yet I despise it because I know it too well.

Before first shots are fired
in the way absence becomes presence
marching for the sake of movement
soles cracked and fraying
half-moon scars etched into dirt
where compliance guarantees failure and
rebellion ensures the same.

The grenades have been armed—this is the sound of surrender
the drawn-out whistle before the blast.
Loaded air too heavy to breathe—the hum of your heart
as it braces for collapse.

A silence louder than bombs.
It's the roar of everything unsaid
breaking its way through your chest.
One last prayer lodged beneath the tongue
louder
louder
louder
until you forget
which one of us
pulled the pin.

East of Eden Blue

Show me anything at all
a parking ticket, chipped nail polish, a breakfast spoon
and I'll romanticize the hell out of it.
Call it art.
Call it survival.
Call it melted-eyeliner dreams
suspended inside a wonky junk drawer.
I don't know much
but I know I've died on more couches than I've kissed on.
My favorite was the pink one
not bubblegum, but that lipstick shade
I wiped off after the funeral
where I swore, I was done writing
or crying
or both
and still left with the tissue box half-gutted
like a ritual I couldn't quit.

(pause. insert blue eyes here.
make them hurt a little.)

Let me live vicariously
through the sliver of light beside your sunglasses
where tiniest rays of blue escape.
East of Eden blue
like Rimbaud's iris
like Cal Trask's might have been
if he listened to Lou Reed's
"Pale Blue Eyes"
when he needs to feel honest
but always skips the bridge

because Lou makes it sound too final.
It's almost laughable
how he names the color so gently.

Maybe he reads Vonnegut
and says it's for the irony
but underlines the saddest lines in private.

I've watched you toss off brilliance like lint
where I've read you like scripture
jealous as hell
wishing I could write half as well
or feel half as little.

Who can afford not to be a poet in times like these?
At least some make a living off the knowing.
The rest of us are just Cal Trask in blue-jean overalls
waiting for a father who won't read our letters—
kids with soft jaws
and louder hearts
loitering on front porches of our own making
letters sweating in our hands
like we still believe in being chosen.

Wolfmilk Heart

The day wakes all red-ribbonry heartsong hawkers
aisle-end garlands weathering confetti
sealing-wax heat in a world of peel-and-stick
shopfronts bright in vitrine fizzlight.

You told me once you hated Valentine's Day.
Not in the cute, candy-script devil-in-pink
easy sneer at Hallmark—but the real thing
more garnet blood-beaded, arterial refusal.

Before cards and butterfat candies, it was all wolfmilk lore.
A Lupercal hush under figs and cliffsides,
old hoofbeat drums pounding through shinlanes
luck as sprint, as skin, as fertility and public hunger.
History didn't vanish.
Just changed its costume.
Slipped backstage in glittered
scarlet shop-talk and pennyshine
our lips tasting dark chocolate tin-sweet syllables of be-mine or
be-maybe.

The thing about love is—it's always time-stamped…
but you couldn't finish the noun.
Said you hated it, but your eyes betrayed you.
Your shoulder blades hinged like theatre doors—enter, exit
a body built for departures and rehearsals for leaving.

Our souls crave union and also obliteration
and sometimes both arrive in the same red-lined envelope

sealed in sugared-saliva and trembling thumbprints
addressed to the part of you that still believes in continuity.

And now you say you hate Valentine's Day
because someone once loved you without irony
and you can't metabolize that kind of humanity.

Run

You sit there wide-eyed, full
of borrowed dreams and other people's expectations
stirring too much sugar into your coffee because
you still think sweetness fixes things.

I want to tell you to run—
to slip out the back door of this quiet life
to cut your hair and disappear into a city
where no one knows your name
and streets are too crowded for regrets to catch up with you.

You look at me with those old-soul brown eyes
searching for hints of happy endings I cannot give you
all I can do is tell you the truth:
it will hurt
more than you ever thought possible.

You will lose things you swore
you couldn't live without
people will promise you forever and mean
until it's no longer convenient.

You will learn the sharp edges of absence
and they will eat away at you, reconstruct you
until you're tougher, more breakable, hyper-aware
a life redrawn inside negative spaces.

You'll spin searing pain into line breaks
and keep betting on tomorrow
even when you swear you're done believing in anything.

I wish I could tell you not to do it
not to hand out pieces of yourself
like flyers
to people who never planned
to stay for the show.

But I know you won't listen.
You never did.

You'll love them anyway
lose them anyway
try to write them into permanence anyway.

So I push back my chair
leave the crumpled bill on the table
and let you believe—for now
there is still time.

That fairytales and forever are something real
and the world is waiting for you with open arms
instead of jagged teeth.

Soon enough, you'll learn the truth.

NORTH BAR

An Eye for an Eye

Somewhere above this swelter
an eye for an eye, right?
You said without saying.
You traded spring for summer
balanced the books
tilted Libra clean off her smug little axis
scattered August's gold teeth across the lawn.

You left me swinging all hurt-stained
heat gnawing my trachea.
Mosquitoes drunk on my blood
wondered if the balance tastes as righteous to you
as the hurt does to me.

I wish you'd make it quicker
instead of this slow hiss of breath
air seeping from a bicycle tire
just enough to make the ride hell
wartime sugar
slow executioner.

Thank you for reminding me
how little I matter
like all those before you.

Great Lakes Incantation in Lieu of Sleep

The calendars become a graveyard now.
Each square a plot.
Red-marker love letters fade from birthdays.
No more glitter-glue pilgrimages
through the fluorescent cathedrals of Target.
Just me in the parking lot
eating gas station cake
pretending it tastes
like the childhood I'd always wanted.

Somewhere between Gratiot and that one bad haircut
I got before meeting Grace
I misplaced my reverence
between parking meters and perfume clouds
down the rinse bowl of this seasons' newest brunette
color spiraling down the drain.
I wonder if she ever knows
this is the only time
I truly feel pretty.

The trees change their colors
like burlesque dancers on strike tired of ornamental seduction.
Even the maples look like they've had enough
to turn ugly and honest.

Everything's ephemeral and
panic attacks don't set their schedules
to nine tidy innings of the Tigers
or astro turf field goals.

It's all piecemeal silent film splices
and that same goddamn scene from *Twilight*
where the girl lies down in a bed of fake plastic violets
as if peace was a meadow
and not something you earned
by surviving the hunt.

Vernors can't cure shit now
but I still drink it
like a sacrament.
Fizz and folklore.
Placebo in a green can
with my grandmother's ghost saying
"shh, it settles the stomach."

I'm sorry for the silence
but I need to lie down.
Please wake me when this lake effect snow
no longer burns.

So It Goes

He works the hush like a switchblade kept polite
palm-flat on the desk, sanctioned smile-smiling
silence is not a civic service but more method.
A soft-lit citizenship of patrons drift through the stacks.
It's always the same story wearing a different jacket
Huxley handing out soma like candy—
don't ask too much, don't feel too hard.

Bright little uniforms and barcode-badges
shelved in a circular cage of logic
each title a mockingbird they forgot to muzzle.
The joke that isn't funny anymore once you're living inside it.
You can leave if you keep quiet.
But if you name it—
they call you the problem, so stay.

He stamps cerulean due dates – or verdicts, you decide
thunk-thunk, goes the small gavel, because he knows how this ends.
He's read the fireman's catechism—
the clean burn, the public bonfires
paper turning to black lace midair
and he knows it doesn't start with matches.
It starts with "just this one title"
then "just this one shelf"
then the soft, neutral phrase: for your own good
as cameras flower in the corners
unblinking proselytizing saints.
He keeps his face unremarkable
as his mind runs contraband routes
between aisles, between Orwellian slogans

there is a code in the cataloging
hiding in decimals and Dewey.
This book beside that book
that paragraph beside this silence
a breadcrumb trail for the ones who still read
like lives depend on it.

A smile and a nice tie as he greets the teen who checks out
dystopias like they're first-aid kits slipped between commas
and smuggled Nor'easters in paperback
And the only punk move left is simple:
keep circulating sentences that don't behave
passing paragraphs spine-to-spine that rewire postures
as we cut our teeth on the pages in our pockets
erupting incisors through the lies.

Ready

Doubt was the first thing I ever learned to trust.
Oldest enemy, oldest roommate.
I knew the sound of its shoes in the hallway
before it ever touched the doorknob.

And of course I didn't come in clean.
I dragged in everything I'd done
and everything I'd tried to wash off in cheap showers
and long walks and spare blankets
of people who meant well.
Some things don't scrub out.
They just dry and crack with you.

When I walked into the room
everybody already knew what part they were supposed to play.
You could see it on their faces:
the ones who cut
the ones who watch the clock
the ones who pretend this is normal.

There were last-minute questions anyway:
who's taking the heart out?
who has to call it?
how long have they got
before the whole thing starts collapsing in on itself?
Okay, they said.
We'll get ready.
As if I hadn't been
this whole time.

an

of it

I love her so muc

ill

he

Fuck It, I'll Be in the Pool

The sky goes vermillion again
or maybe it's just the reflection of
my blistered-skin sunburn
or another burning building in a country I can't save.

The world, apparently, ends in fire or ice—
Frost couldn't seem to pick.
It's a hundred degrees in June
the planet's in hospice
but I shaved my legs anyway.

They ask me to keep my glass half-full
but it ruptured the night they voted yes on poison
and called it progress
sometime around the third once-in-a-lifetime wildfire.

I gave up recycling when they started arresting librarians
and submerged—cause the water's warm
and the earth is boiling.

The ladder is rust-bitten
Hawaiian Tropic is beading at the base of my neck
like holy oil
all coconut and capitalism.

So fine—drop the bomb and let the power grids fail.
If everything's melting away anyway
what's one more woman walking out into the deep end
skin slick, suit clinging, fresh out of illusions saying
"Fuck it, I'll be in the pool."

Lick Your Wounds

They only call when something's broken.
When a pipe coughs grit into the sink.
When the furnace cuts its warmth mid-sentence
and the house goes mean with cold.
When the train stalls at 4:07 a.m.
and strangers make a temporary congregation.

No one remembers the hands that kept it running.
The ones who showed up early
thumbs split from cardboard
knees damp from basement cement
coffee gone metallic in the cup holder
because today didn't have room for caffeinated crisis.

I move through their world like incidental ink
my name typed into a form, then backspaced
and whited-out.

I'm the person they mistake for furniture:
only noticed when I'm missing, or uncomfortable
or rearranged
only addressed when something won't open
won't start, won't hold up.

I have been the hinge-pin that screamed
and still did its job
the towel pressed into a leak
until the ceiling learned to behave.

I am the blank square on the wall
where a frame used to hang
the smudge of ochre on a doorway
after paint dries
proof of a hand that steadied the whole house
without anyone naming it a rite.

And when I'm finally alone
I don't pray.
I do what animals do:
I lick my wounds
swallow the iron taste of it
and finally learn how to set up
that voicemail I've been putting off
because knowing how to leave
isn't the same as being gone
but it's a start.

The Short Days of Winter

Those short winter days had this weird, low-budget holiness to them. The light never really showed up—just washed-out colors like somebody turned the world down to half-volume. Even the snow, once pale-white glitter, looked like it wanted to be someplace else and not all piled up here.
The air would get at us nipping our faces, or our knuckles, until it crossed that line and started to feel almost good. Do you remember how our skin would go red, fingers stinging, ears burning, and somehow that hurt made us feel more alive than anything inside ever did? Our arms and legs lit up with that stupid, stubborn warmth, like our bodies were saying, *fine then, we're still here.*

Most nights it felt like we were sprinting through tunnels with nothing but dark at our backs, maybe a little ahead of us too—but we kept going anyway, just to get to whatever light was left at the end of the block.

That was the whole thing back then—
run the dark
just to stumble back into the light together.

They Still Want the Old Songs

There are nights when you feel like
you're lip-syncing your own life.
Words leave your mouth
but they don't belong to you anymore.
They're artifacts of a self that once believed in reverberation.
It's a strange form of isolation
to be applauded for what no longer feels true.
To watch people sing along
to the spirit of who you were.
You think about the futility of revolt.

Some days you believe repetition is redemption
that if you say the same line again and again
it might evolve into truth.

Alienation is supposedly modern
but you know it's ancient.
It's the soul's quiet refusal to be sold for recognition.

Art no longer heals you
it preserves you
like formaldehyde.
You can still see remnants
but it no longer sustains.

They still want the old songs.
The ones written in the fever of twenty
when irony still passes for prayer.
They want the myth that never grows up.

You watch them recite the chorus
like it's gospel
unwilling to meet the version of you
that outlived the key change.

And still, some part of you wants to be beautiful for them.
To keep faith there's meaning
in saying the same lines over and over
until they're finally proud of you
or nostalgic enough
to mistake endurance for grace.

Lately you don't know what to keep writing anymore.
Every sentence feels embalmed.

Maybe that's love
or its afterimage—
to keep performing tenderness
long after it's gone
to feed the myth that raised you
even as it drains your name
back into the void.

Bright-Eyed

And he makes me feel something
a little tremor, a faint ping of presence
just enough to tilt the day askew

And it makes me want to write down
every absurd, trembling, meaningless feeling that
arrives mid-sentence, rearranges the interior
It's ridiculous, the way it sends me
grabbing for a pen like a drowning thing
I'm on first attempts at second drafts
trying to write every uneven
barely formed impulse before it dissipates
as if words might finally pin down
whatever keeps shuddering awake

And it makes me want to be a better writer
or at least someone who deserves this feeling.
Not in the noble sense, just sharper
less afraid of the thing that wants to come through

And it makes me want to erase my memory
burn old wiring
that taught me to flinch at anything good
kindness is a counterfeit bill
tenderness is ambush
both preludes to loss

And it makes me want to
God knows what

Disappear
Begin again
Walk into the sea, finally come out clean

And I hate that I care
and I care that I hate this
private hell of
small inferno
looping under bone

I keep gravitating towards patterns
brilliance, damage, the whole
beautiful-wreck-perimeter
As if repeating the injury
might finally rewrite the origin

Part of me wants to drop it
just to stop the shaking
and part of me wants to cage it
because I don't trust myself
not to ruin it

I fear I've already misnamed it
called it love
called it something it never promised itself to be
and I'm scared that one day I'll lose it completely

And I'm trying
to learn how to take a compliment
without feeling it scorch the inside of my palms
bracing for burns
scanning escape routes

hearing old rooms
where kindness was a trick hinge
and praise the first step toward disappearance

I can feel the glitch
the instinct to destroy the good thing
before it destroys me
failing

And I don't know if that's progress
or just another kind of combustion
but it feels like truth
that there are more honest things about me
than the wreckages
I leave intact

Split the Difference

The speakers of the Traverse City coffee shop
are leaking out nothing but autopsies.
A lone barista has the inventory of the unloved on repeat—
Elliott Smith with a dash of Mitski
and one weary Pearl Jam relic breaking through—a reminder
that "Better Man" was never about becoming one, but about
learning to sip bitterness politely while someone else's grief
plays on repeat.

And I tell myself now
that I no longer want to be loved
because the alternative is admitting
I still do—and let's face it
that shit never saved anyone
except the people we wrote it for.

I've always admired those who write lyrics
it's just poetry with better PR.
We split the difference:
but you get to sing it in a voice that gets you laid.
And let's not kid ourselves
we're both taxidermists for the same animal
slicing open old pain and stuffing it with lights, sawdust and
string.
You just add reverb.
I sprinkle in some shame.

I don't want to be loved, I say.
But what I mean is:
I'm tired of begging in ways I can still pretend to be poems.
I don't want to be saved. Just named.

And every time I hit the refrain
and it asks me what I want from it
I say *nothing*.
I say *forget it*.
When what I mean is:
Say *I was real*.
Say *I was music*
because I've heard you sing it before in other towns
to other people
that didn't have to
make their bruises
look poetic.

GROUND

—We stay up through decades picking up whatever falls
saying, we still want the world—
even now.

Small Mercy

A friend with kind eyes and calloused fingers
sang "Madame George"
from the van's front seat
window cracked just enough
for the cold to crawl inside with the chorus.
It reached me
low and sideways, through the static
a voice like sugar on a burn
like someone remembered your name
and said it slow.

You say goodbye
in that song
over and over
and it still doesn't feel finished.
the kind of goodbye
before you know who's going.

It wasn't for me
but I heard it
the way his voice dipped
on something about throwing pennies from bridges
and I thought
yeah, I've done that
not with coins
but with pieces of myself
I never expected to get back
small copper weights so familiar.
It hit soft

like a match struck underwater
a brief light inside the dark
I never quite learned how to carry.

I didn't cry
just let the words
settle into me
like they belonged there.

A pause. A held note
and then that line
the one about loving the love you love to love—
of course
that's what we all do.
We chase the shape of connection
even when it's only
the mirror of our own longing
flashed back through someone else's voice.

And grief, yes, an old friend
but quieter now, curious
and more willing to sit at the far end of the table
never healed
but briefly still
like when I leave with
my heart tucked into a hug
I pretend might not be the last.

I always say I'll be back
and maybe I will
but not all of me travels home.

He sang, and it wasn't for me
not to me
but it passed through me
like low tide pulling at the underside
that part of me that still remembers
how to listen
without flinching
or feeling forgotten
after closing chords.

The wound in me
keeps rehearsing its lines
but tonight, inside a minute-long message
from someone who didn't know
came not just a song
but a small mercy.

Swimlight

A tarp
peeled back
silk from a secret
undressed from the
film of winter
flensed clean
the water blinked awake
half sunlight
half memory
it remembered me
        wet hair
            stuck to cheek
                peachflesh
      bitten
         to the stone
the peach tree
leaning
blushboned
sweetburdened
    like it knows
    what it means
       to flower
          beside thirst
skin warm
the summer's always been
inside me
turquoise wet
chlorine musk
lifting up from the water's edge

come now
it said
come new
like seduction
but older
the water remembers
every version of me
destructionheavy
joystarved
arms flung wide
in old laughter
touches my back
like prayer or possession
blue today poured back into blue
barefoot I step
ceruleanlipped
chlorinetoothed
I am
a new Eve
offering myself back
to an Eden
that could drown me
or hold me
this—baptism of body
a weathered hymn
a skin-toned psalm
I slip beneath the waterline
like a woman
stepping into her own name
for the first
and final
time

Seven Autumns Later

I measure the years now not in clemency
but in dead wood.
How September arrives again
pocketing daylight.

People say autumn is glorious
but it's just trees learning how to die publicly.
Everything you love gets brighter
just before it falls apart.

It was this irony that pulled me through while
writing elegies on the backsides of mounting bills
emotional or otherwise—
tucked inside the library books I never returned
but meant to.

Sometimes I loved just for the noise
and sometimes just for the hush.
The unclaimed luggage of everyone I touched
crowded the compartments of my chest.

So now you ask me
after all these collapses and counterfeit dawns
if I can look back and say I did my best?

Reader, I confess:
I slept inside other people's metaphors
when my own house was on fire.

I watch the trees abandon what's no longer vital as they shed
their leaves the way I try to shed memories

but memory is a root system:
When you cut off the crown
the old hunger shoots up throught the dirt.

Perseverance is an artform
a blueprint, a thing you learn by doing
and rarely gets the credit it deserves.

I look out my window and see the trees stripping down
without shame—yellow slips, pale arms, the works
and I think to myself, "why not me?"

In the hush before November frost
I forgive that version of myself
who could only hold onto anything
but severance
and I can say now, with seven September's distance
I honestly did my best.

Set It Down

You've been waiting for me
under the kitchen drawer that sticks on the left side
lined with *Saturday Evening Post* pages from 1954
Norman Rockwell Americana curling yellowed at the edges.

A cryptex rested
dials smudged with the fingerprints
both of hope and hesitation.
Fibonacci spirals of 1, 1, 2, 3, 5, 8.

I loved you even in the quietest of mornings
which is how you know it was real.
But lifting you now feels different
heavier somehow
as if I still haven't learned
not to ask questions
I don't want the answers to.

The room receives January's whiskey-stained light
pooling amber through the window and
traces the geometry of a parquet floor that no longer adds up.

I rotate the dials with cold precision
and think of all the times I forced
the lock, the silence, the shape of fate.
And now—
now I've solved it.

The click is gentle but deliberate.
I hesitate.
Maybe ignorance is bliss.
Maybe the answers were never mine to find.
Maybe the questions were never about you
and always
about me.

Tonight is yesterday
and I am the same as I was before
only I hold emptiness differently now.

A thing I thought that would save me
when all it ever needed me to do was wait
and learn how
to set it down.

Transatlanticism

Beckett once whispered to us in the dark—
perhaps no one is coming
and maybe that's the tragic beauty of it all.

As we stand, poised on the edge
thirsting for anything
to pull us back from the chaos
the senseless swirl where we seek meaning
only to find that
we know nothing
and perhaps we never did.

Yet, we pause in vain
watch the world unfold
in the slow semaphore or unfinished transmissions
like dreamers waiting on telegrams
from a distant past
arms outstretched like the old Chappe telegraph
reaching across time and space
hoping perhaps for a reply
that may never come.

The tragedy isn't in the waiting
but in the elegant reach
the quiet persistence
the way we stand
desperately poised between despair and desire
clinging to the belief that someday
a world will answer back
even if it never does.

The Long Way Home

We walked the long way home
because neither one of us wanted the house to arrive too soon.
The alternative was standing still long enough
for the truth to climb into our mouths.

You kept your hands in your pockets
like you were nursing a wounded quail, hush-winged so the hounds
wouldn't nose it out
I kept my own hands busy, sifting nothing but wind
and that's how we survived it.

Your shoulder brushed mine, not on accident
as I idled a line of beer caps glittering alongside the curb
like little ruined crowns.
You stared down at me and I wanted your eyes the way parched fields
want rainstorms.

Your voice was doing that slow, human thing—turning pain into those
songs with the same three chords that break your heart
turning panic into jokes you didn't fully believe.

We were good at being brave.
If I could have pulled the heat
out of the wire—left only the shape of it
harmless, humming—I would have stayed
the way people share intrepid breaths without counting.
I would have taken the hit for you, wiped the salt
from your eyes with my own mistakes.

I would have handed you every peace offering I had—
olive trees of slow green
sentences that take years to mean what they mean.

I watched you walk ahead of me
as you stood in front of your gate and
left you my believing, even when I could no longer stand inside it.
(Truth is, I can't sit inside any uncomfortable thing long enough)
You practiced a new address
let it settle in at the back of your throat.

And then I did the cruelest gentlest thing:
I memorized the weight of your voice
to carry with me
so my ghost
wasn't walking home
alone

Orange Flood

The road outside was evening-warm, slate-gray, smelling of rain that had nowhere better to be than here falling between the two of us. I found myself riding shotgun in the peeled-orange husk of a '60s Volkswagen Beetle.

You always said the music was the most important thing. You had already yanked out the original radio and soldered a tape deck you found at the scrapyard in its place. Your blanched palms drummed the dry-rotted steering wheel as it flooded the dash speaker popcorn fidelity, but every downstroke was crisp as new tin. You smiled at me with that trademark grin that I knew as both salvation and trouble. I felt the hum of the transformer pole travel up my arm and understood why sixteen-year-olds swear on forever: because the weld still held fire and the song hadn't ended in tragedy but instead with soothing clicks when the cassette flipped sides.

The floor had given up five seasons ago, but you didn't mind the rusted crater, said you'd fix it tomorrow. Later we'd find out that was the only thing holding it all together. You let the car coast past the water tower where pigeons slept, past the Speedway and 7-11 where the tires sliced a rain-fat puddle and water geysered up, anointing the back of my jeans. You laughed so hard the steering column shook and you blushed the same shade of tangerine as the paint. I still laugh when I think of it. The next day when you were welding sheet-steel fireflies into the floorpan and killed the torch and that cherry of the rod went dark, you noticed me mid-stare and jokingly asked why I always hauled that dog-eared copy of *The Mutant King* in my back pocket. I quickly shot back, "Because I'm studying the understudy."

Some nights, thirty years off, I still wake thinking water is climbing my calves and feeling alive again is encapsulated somewhere inside an orange shell roaring over puddles with sparks refusing to die—just roaming metal to metal until another body of floodwater invites them home.

Unripen

The peach tree dumped more unripe peaches in the yard this year as if it
too, had grown tired of trying to ripen things with time.
We were out there gathering what it had decided to give up—
plastic bag tied round your arm with
years stretched behind you like shadows across the wet grass.

I think I was afraid when I was ten, you said.
And I thought
So was I.
Just older.

From the deck speaker we heard the Counting Crows singing about lions
and lambs like someone else was
narrating us years before you were born.
The way they slip truth into the chorus always breaks me.

Your tenacity makes me think of Camus—the idea that even in the hard
center of winter, there's a heat in us that can't be extinguished.

What if the calendar soured in the sun
just days, just debt, just lists of what never ripened?
The tree keeps weeping bitter fruit.
The hands gathering them are older
but not wiser—just more tired.

Grief isn't the hour they leave.
It's the years that follow
when no one else shows up to clean the yard.
Only you. Only me.

And I remember how we stopped drawing lines between sleep
and survival sometime that first year.
Days I sat fully clothed inside the bathtub
and watched the mirror fog over
tracing my limits in steam
until they wept themselves back into water.

You learned to live inside the residue.
Grief wasn't sacred
It was mundane.
It made me better at reading the room.
It lived inside a T-shirt I didn't wash for three months because
it still smelled like before.

It lived inside me, it became me.
To fall asleep was surrender.
To stay awake was evidence
you once mattered to someone and
pain could prove it.

You learned to accept that love is often unspectacular, that
epiphanies happen at CVS under fluorescent lighting.
Through every half-birthday
I ached while watching my sons become men.
I still feel like a child waiting at the edge of loss, and I know
that eventually grief will make poets of everyone.

You're taller than me now
and we both pretend that doesn't make me cry.

Today was just a bowl of spoiled peaches
and the sound of your voice
lower than I remember

saying, "It's weird to remember."
And me saying
"It's weirder not to."

The music cracked on again
about staying up way too late
and I thought
We do.
We have.
We will.

We stay up through decades
picking up whatever falls.
Saying *we still want the world*
even now.
But behind a cautious smile
remains a quiet question—
Will they leave us, too?

Love Field

I had that dream about you again last night.
You said, "Meet me at Love Field because I want to break open
like the world did that one day in Dallas."
And I come looking for you
like a country that lost its future—
too slow, too late
still hoping the motorcade turns around.

I drove there like it mattered.
You're the only person I'd do this for.
The only one who ever made me feel like
maybe I wasn't already past saving.

We lied down with our backs pressed flat against
the hot tarmac clinging to our shirts
and watched those metal herons scrape open the sky.
I thought how bizarre it is
that anything this heavy could still take flight.
You turned to me and said
"It's louder when they leave."
And I didn't ask what you meant
because I already know.

I said, "You think these are still the ones from '63?"
You laughed, which was the whole point.
I think you knew I don't really care about the planes.

You traced circles on the inside of my wrist
like it was a map that could take you anywhere
but here.

We talked about how the ancient Greeks had so many words
for ruin and so few for salvation.
Even that was conditional: *sōtēria*—to save
but only if there's something left to hold.

Everything in me wants to be translated
like opening pages of *War and Peace*
each name kept intact, each contradiction left standing.

You said you knew me better than anyone
but you never read the footnotes.
I'm not what you think.
I'm worse.
I'm better.
I'm trying.
I'm not a metaphor for anything
except maybe aftermath.

And then we kissed
not to fix what broke in Dallas
but because escape tastes better
with your mouth on mine.

Soft Apocalypse

I passed a laundromat
where clothes spun in absolution
and I thought about forgiveness—
how it's not something you give
but something you carry
like a pebble in your shoe
you forget it's there
and keep walking anyway.

That, I think
is what peace feels like
a quiet ache
of surviving
without asking for permission.

Someone left a guitar pick
in the coin return tray—
I took it like a sign
even though I barely play.

The sky was leaking pollen and prophecy—
this, I thought, is becoming:
a slow unravel in the frozen food aisle
while "Mr. Tambourine Man" plays
and someone buys bottled water
like salvation comes
in the shape of a barcode.

I kept walking—
past the fence lined with sun-faded pink flamingos

past a mailbox jammed with ransom notes and
catalogs nobody needs.
Back to the old house
where nothing had moved since '97.

Dust as second skin
coating the pool table
green felt gone gray
pockets full of silence
and secrets that stay buried
even when we didn't.
And your voice still hums
when the fridge kicks on
or when I almost fall asleep
and remember you never said goodbye.
Still, I keep a toothbrush by the window
in case hope wants to stay the night.

This isn't the apocalypse—
but it's something close.
Where no one notices
except the girl at the corner store
who asks if I'm okay
and doesn't believe me when I say I am
as the phone wires shake above our heads
like violin strings mid-note—
almost beautiful
but just as easily broken.

And when the end comes
it'll wear your ex's sweatshirt
and sit on the edge of the bed
like someone who used to know you.

And I'll be there
with a copy of *Play the Devil* in my back pocket
and a list of things I loved
torn up and folded inside of a locket.

Boots full of river water
passing sparrows
rehearsing eulogies
in the alley behind the gas station.

I'll stop between the motor oil
and dollar romance novels
wondering once more
if you remember
the thing I never said out loud.

And I'll write one last poem
on a crumpled-up receipt
and swear

I didn't
write it
for
you.

ACKNOWLEDGEMENTS

I would like to thank the writers who offered their kind words of praise in the form of blurbs. It means more than I can say to have this book met with such generosity. I admire you all so much, it feels a bit surreal.

To my editor-in-chief—thank you for listening to me overthink (everything), for your time and patience and help organizing the chaos.

To the people and places who supported or inspired any part of this—this book is a love letter, in more ways than one, to you.

To the great music and musicians who scored the playlist of these years and the memories inside them—thank you for giving me language when I didn't yet have my own.

And to you, the reader—thank you for choosing a book named *Live Wire*. You have excellent taste in questionable decisions. In all seriousness, thank you for letting this collection keep you company for a while. Thank you for reading, I hope you enjoyed it.

MEET THE AUTHOR

Amy Laessle-Morgan is a poet based in Southeast Michigan. Her work has appeared in *Gypsophila Art & Literary Magazine*, *Sterling Script*, *Artifex Literary Magazine*, *Livina Press*, *Squirrel Cane Press*, *Azarão Lit Journal*, *Major 7th Magazine*, *Two Key Customs* and *Crying Heart Press* where she also received the Editor's Choice Award (2026) and is the author of her debut poetry collection, *East Coast Heartbreak* (Neon Sparrow Press, 2024).

When she's not writing, she enjoys photography, listening to records and playing bass guitar — not well, but with feeling. You can find more of her work on Instagram @ultramarine_poetry.

OTHER BOOKS BY AMY LAESSLE-MORGAN

EAST COAST HEARTBREAK

Amy Laessle-Morgan's debut poetry collection, *East Coast Heartbreak*, traces the delicate path between heartbreak and hope, where love persists despite the weight of profound loss. Drawing deeply from her personal journey, Amy explores the fragility of the heart, torn between longing for the past and yearning for an unknown future. Amidst the chaos, healing and beauty slowly surface, much like the first light of dawn rising over the Atlantic.

www.ingramcontent.com/pod-product-compliance
Lightning Source LLC
LaVergne TN
LVHW090522110826
845146LV00003B/954

* 9 7 9 8 2 1 8 8 9 8 5 4 0 *